Glor

GW00859565

God

Obedient Lives from the Bible

Glorifying God

Obedient Lives from the Bible

Carine Mackenzie

CF4·K

10 9 8 7 6 5 4 3 2 1
© Copyright 2013 Carine Mackenzie
ISBN: 978-1-78191-124-2

Published in 2013 by
Christian Focus Publications,
Geanies House, Fearn, Tain
Ross-shire, IV20 1TW,
Great Britain

Cover design by Paul Lewis
Illustrations by Fred Apps
Printed and bound by Bell and Bain, Glasgow

The Scripture version used throughout this book is The King James or the author's own paraphrase.

For our grandchildren:
Lydia, Esther, Philip,
Lois, Jack, Marianne,
Isobel and Elizabeth

Contents

Putting God First

We are always making choices – which T-shirt to wear – which flavour of crisps to buy. Sometimes we have good reasons for the choice we make. Often it is just a matter of preference. Many of the choices we make are not very important but some are extremely important.

God gave us the Ten Commandments as guidelines for our daily living. He wants us to obey his commands. His first commandment states, 'Thou shalt have no other gods before me' (Exodus 20:3).

When Joshua was an old man, he gathered the leaders of Israel together at Shechem to tell them God's message. They were reminded of God's goodness to them in times past. He delivered them from slavery in Egypt and gave them the Promised Land. They were presented with a vitally important choice. To put away the gods that their forefathers used to serve. Choose not to serve the same false gods that the local people the Amorites serve. Instead, 'fear the LORD and serve him in sincerity and truth.'

'Choose you this day whom you will serve,' Joshua told the people, 'but as for me and my house, we will serve the LORD.'

We have that important choice too. The Lord God Jehovah, the God of the Bible, is the only God. We should worship him only. He tolerates no rivals. You may hear about other gods and religions in school. Jehovah is not merely the best god; he is in a class of his own – the one and only true God.

Shadrach, Meshach and Abednego were captives in Babylon. King Nebuchadnezzar told the people to worship his golden statue or else they would be thrown into a burning fiery furnace. Shadrach, Meshach and Abednego refused to bow down. They obeyed God's first commandment. 'Thou shalt have no other gods before me.'

Nebuchadnezzar was angry and heated the furnace seven times hotter than usual. When the three men were thrown in, Nebuchadnezzar was amazed. 'We threw three men into the fire,' he exclaimed, 'but I see four men walking unhurt. The fourth looks like the son of God.'

Shadrach, Meshach and Abednego walked out of the fire and there was not even the smell of burning on their clothes. Nebuchadnezzar was impressed. 'Blessed be God who saved his servants. They trusted in him and risked their lives in order to worship the one true God.'

We can ask God to give us the courage and commitment to put him first. The first puzzle on page 13 will show you what Jesus says should be first in your life.

Bible Verse

And God spake all these
words, saying,
I am the LORD thy God, which have
brought thee out of the land of
Egypt, out of the house of bondage.
Thou shalt have no other gods
before me.
Exodus 20:1-3

Bible Search 1

The missing words from these verses will show you what Jesus says should be most important in Matthew 6:33.

1. But if from thence thou shalt _____ the LORD thy God, thou shalt find him, if thou seek him with all thy heart and with all thy soul (Deuteronomy 4:29).

2. And the gospel must _____ be published among all nations (Mark 13:10).

3. Who knoweth whether thou art come to ____ _____ for such a time as this? (Esther 4:14)

4. And the spirit ___   _____ moved upon the face of the waters (Genesis 1:2).

5. His soul shall dwell at ease; _____   _____ seed shall inherit the earth (Psalm 25:13).

6. Follow after _____, godliness, faith, love, patience, meekness (1 Timothy 6:11).

Bible Search 2

Find the words missing from the verses. The initials of your answers will spell out an important message.

1. Let us hear the conclusion of the _____ matter: Fear God, and keep his commandments. (Ecclesiastes 12:13).

2. Then saith Jesus unto him, Get thee hence, Satan: for it is written, Thou shalt worship the Lord thy God, and him _____ shalt thou serve (Matthew 4:10).

3. Serve the LORD with fear, and _____ with trembling (Psalm 2:11).

4. For all have _____ , and come short of the glory of God (Romans 3:23).

5. What doth the LORD require of thee, but to do justly, and to love mercy, and to walk _____ with thy God? (Micah 6:8)

6. There is none good but one, that is, God: but if thou wilt enter _____ life, keep the commandments (Matthew 19:17).

7. Serve the LORD with gladness: come before his _____ with singing (Psalm 100:2).

8. Be it known unto thee, O king, that we will not serve thy gods, nor worship the _____ image which thou hast set up (Daniel 3:18).

9. And the people said unto Joshua, The LORD our God will we serve, and his voice will we _____ (Joshua 24:24).

10. In all thy ways acknowledge him, and he shall _____ thy paths (Proverbs 3:6).

Worship from the Heart

Why do you go to church? Is it because your parents say that you must? Do you just go to see your friends? Or perhaps you enjoy singing. Some people go to hear good preaching, and to learn more about the Bible.

The most important reason for going to church is to worship God. Our attendance at church is primarily for God. He has told us in his Word how we should do this. God's second commandment clearly states that we must not make any idols or statues to represent God. We should worship him in the way that pleases him, as he has told us in his Word. God is a Spirit and those who worship him must worship him in spirit and in truth.

God's people have fallen into the sin of wrong worship or idolatry many times. Even when Moses was up Mount Sinai meeting with God, the people became impatient. 'Make us gods,' they demanded of Aaron, Moses' brother. 'We don't know what has happened to Moses.'

Aaron did as they asked. He melted down their golden earrings and formed the shape of a calf. Then they worshipped it and had a big feast. Moses was so angry when he saw this. He took the calf, ground it to powder and made the people drink it sprinkled on water. Moses then confessed the sin of the people.

On another occasion on the wilderness journey, the children of Israel were complaining yet again against God. God sent fierce serpents to the camp and many people were bitten and died. 'We have sinned against God,' the rest confessed to Moses. 'Please pray that God would take the snakes away.'

Moses prayed for the people and God told him, 'Make a bronze serpent and set it up on a pole. Whenever anyone who has been bitten, looks at this bronze serpent, he will live.'

The bronze serpent was God's appointed means of curing the people who had been bitten. But in years to come the people started to worship this bronze serpent. When King Hezekiah became King of Judah he removed the altars and broke the images that the people worshipped. He broke in pieces the bronze serpent that Moses had made. It was only a piece of bronze. What had started as a God-given blessing, had become a curse, causing the people to commit the sin of idolatry.

We may not worship bronze serpents or other kinds of statues, but if anything takes the place of God in our hearts, then we are guilty of idolatry too. Even blessings given to us by God, like church, or a preacher or a writer, can be given too high a place in our hearts and so become an idol.

Obedience to God's Word should be our priority, worshipping him from the heart not just with our lips. We should respond to God's mercy, by loving him because he first loved us.

Bible Verses

Thou shalt not make unto thee any graven image, or any likeness of any thing that is in heaven above, or that is in the earth beneath, or that is in the water under the earth. Thou shalt not bow down thyself to them, nor serve them: for I the LORD thy God am a jealous God, visiting the iniquity of the fathers upon the children unto the third and fourth generation of them that hate me. And shewing mercy unto thousands of them that love me, and keep my commandments.
Exodus 20:4-6

Wherefore, my dearly beloved, flee
from idolatry.
1 Corinthians 10:14

Little children, keep yourselves from
idols. Amen.
1 John 5:21

In that day a man shall cast his
idols of silver, and his idols of
gold, which they made each one for
himself to worship, to the moles and
to the bats.
Isaiah 2:20

Bible Search 3

Find the missing words. The initials of your answers will spell out the sin mentioned in the story.

1. I am the LORD: that is my name: and my glory will I not give to another, neither my praise to graven _____ (Isaiah 42:8).

2. Wherefore, my _____ beloved, flee from idolatry (1 Corinthians 10:14).

3. Behold, to _____ is better than sacrifice, and to hearken than the fat of rams (1 Samuel 15:22).

4. This people draweth nigh unto me with their mouth, and honoureth me with their _____ ; but their heart is far from me (Matthew 15:8).

5. What thing soever I command you, observe to do it: thou shalt not _____ thereto, nor diminish from it (Deuteronomy 12:32).

6. For they themselves shew of us what manner of entering in we had unto you, and how ye _____

to God from idols to serve the living and true God (1 Thessalonians 1:9).

7. For _____ is as the sin of witchcraft, and stubbornness is as iniquity and idolatry (1 Samuel 15:23).

8. Know ye not, that to whom ye _____ yourselves servants to obey, his servants ye are to whom ye obey; whether of sin unto death, or of obedience unto righteousness? (Romans 6:16)

Respect for God's Name

Do you know what your name means? Every name has a meaning and it can be interesting to look up in a book or on the internet the meaning of your name and the names of your friends and family. It can be very hurtful and upsetting if someone calls us a nasty name.

The name of God is very important and the third Commandment teaches us to treat God's name with respect and honour and warns us of the danger of using God's name wrongly. God's name tells us what he is like and all that he does. On Mount Sinai the Lord descended in a cloud and stood with Moses, and 'proclaimed the name of the LORD' (Exodus 34:5). He proclaimed, 'The LORD God, merciful and gracious, long-suffering and abundant in goodness and truth, keeping mercy for thousands, forgiving iniquity and transgression and sin and that will by no means clear the guilty' (Exodus 34:6-7). What an amazing description of God's name. God's name is holy because God is holy. We should 'praise the name of the LORD for his name alone is excellent' (Psalm 148:13).

God's name can be misused or taken in vain, when people use God's name in conversation without thinking, just as an exclamation of surprise or horror. People blaspheme God's name when they defy him

and cast doubt on his character. Rabshakeh said outrageous things against the LORD to Hezekiah the king. He mocked Hezekiah for trusting in the LORD (2 Kings 19). This was dreadful blasphemy.

We can honour God's name by giving him praise and thanksgiving. 'I will praise thy name, O LORD, for it is good' (Psalm 54:6). God loves his people to call on his name in prayer asking for help and believing his Word. We can honour God by reading his Word and thinking about it. The Lord hears when we speak together about him. A book of remembrance was written before him for them that feared the LORD and that thought upon his name (Malachi 3:16).

Bible Verse

Thou shalt not take the name of the LORD thy God in vain; for the LORD will not hold him guiltless that taketh his name in vain.
Exodus 20:7

Bible Search 4

Find the missing words. The initial letters of your answers will spell out a description of God's name found in Proverbs chapter 18.

1. Sing unto the LORD, bless his name: shew forth his

   _____ from day to day (Psalm 96:2).

2. Let them praise thy great and _____ name;

   for it is holy (Psalm 99:3).

3. But let all those that put their trust in thee

   _____ : ... let them also that love thy

   name be joyful in thee (Psalm 5:11).

4. Give unto the LORD the glory due unto his name:

   bring an _____ and come before him

   (1 Chronicles 16:29).

5. O let not the oppressed return ashamed: let the

   poor and _____ praise thy name (Psalm 74:21).

6. God said moreover unto Moses, Thus shalt thou

   say unto the children of Israel, The LORD God of

your fathers ... hath sent me unto you: this is my name for ever, and this is my memorial unto all _____(Exodus 3:15).

7. I will ... and praise thy name for thy lovingkindness and for thy _____ : for thou hast magnified thy word above all thy name (Psalm 138:2).

8. Neither is there salvation in any _____: for there is none other name under heaven given among men, whereby we must be saved (Acts 4:12).

9. And I will _____ on thy name; for it is good before thy saints (Psalm 52:9).

10. Praise the LORD, call upon his name, declare his doings among the people, make mention that his name is _____ (Isaiah 12:4).

11. In thy name shall they rejoice all the day: and in thy _____ shall they be exalted (Psalm 89:16).

God's Special Day

Are you looking forward to celebrating your birthday? Perhaps you will have a favourite meal or go for an outing with friends. That special day only comes round once a year, but God has given us a very special day every week.

God has told us to remember the Sabbath to keep it holy. One day in seven is to be different from the other six days. Six days for work and one day to be kept specially for worship and rest. God started this pattern for work and rest from the beginning of time. He created the world in six days and rested on the seventh – not because he was tired, but to show his people what he knew to be best for them.

Until the resurrection of Jesus Christ, the seventh day of the week (our Saturday) was the Sabbath, the day of rest. The risen Lord Jesus appeared to his disciples on the first day of the week which we call Sunday and again on the following Sunday. So now the first day of the week, Sunday or the Lord's Day is the Christian Sabbath.

How are we to keep God's special day holy? We are to lay aside our normal daily work and leisure pursuits which are quite permissible on other days. We are to honour God by worshipping him in public and at home. This is not only for God's glory but for our good.

Glorifying God

Jesus kept God's law perfectly. He went to the synagogue on the Sabbath to worship. One Sabbath day in Capernaum he healed a man who had an evil demon in him. He then went to his friend Simon Peter's house where he healed Simon Peter's mother-in-law who was suffering with a fever. She was able to get out of bed at once and serve the food. Later in the evening, Jesus healed many other people. He was not idle on the Sabbath – he worshipped God the Father, he preached, he helped the sick and ate food with friends.

Some work has to be done on the Lord's Day. Nurses, policemen, ambulance drivers and people doing other essential services have to be on duty every day. What they do is called a work of necessity and mercy. It would be cruel to refuse to do that work. The particular work done on the Lord's Day could not have been done the day before and could not wait until Monday.

When we treat the Lord's Day as a special day we give God glory. It is his day and we should honour him by obeying his commandment. It is also a benefit and a blessing to us, physically, mentally and spiritually. God has made us in such a way that we need rest every day and one day in seven.

32

The Sabbath (or Lord's Day) is also a regular reminder to God's people that he has set them apart as his own possession. 'Ye are not your own. For ye are bought with a price' (1 Corinthians 6:19-20). What a price! The precious blood of Christ was shed to pay the redemption price for God's own people. He is worthy of our praise, worship and remembrance of him and his day.

Bible Verses

Remember the sabbath day, to keep it holy. Six days shalt thou labour, and do all thy work: But the seventh day is the sabbath of the LORD thy God: in it thou shalt not do any work, thou, nor thy son, nor thy daughter, thy manservant, nor thy maidservant, nor thy cattle, nor thy stranger that is within thy gates: For in six days the LORD made heaven and earth, the sea, and all that in them is, and rested the seventh day: wherefore the LORD blessed the sabbath day, and hallowed it.

Exodus 20:8-11

Then said Jesus unto them, I will ask you one thing; Is it lawful on the sabbath days to do good, or to do evil? to save life, or to destroy it?
Luke 6:9

And when the sabbath day was come, he began to teach in the synagogue: and many hearing him were astonished, saying, From whence hath this man these things? and what wisdom is this which is given unto him, that even such mighty works are wrought by his hands?
Mark 6:2

Bible Search 5

Find the missing words in the verses. The initials of the correct answers will spell out the subject of the story.

1. Verily my sabbaths ye shall keep: for it is a sign between me and you _____ your generations (Exodus 31:13).

2. Remember ... that the LORD thy God brought thee out thence through a mighty _____ and by a stretched out arm: therefore the LORD thy God commanded thee to keep the sabbath day (Deuteronomy 5:15).

3. Then I contended with the nobles of Judah, and said unto them, What _____ thing is this that ye do, and profane the sabbath day? (Nehemiah 13:17)

4. Six days shalt thou _____ and do all thy work: But the seventh day is the sabbath of the LORD thy God (Exodus 20:9-10).

5. I was in the Spirit on the Lord's day, and heard behind me a great voice, as of a trumpet, saying,

I am Alpha and _____ , the first and the last (Revelation 1:10-11).

6. And God blessed the seventh day, and sanctified it: because that in it he had _____ from all his work which God created and made (Genesis 2:3).

7. If thou turn away thy foot from the sabbath, from doing thy pleasure on my holy day; and call the sabbath a _____ ... (Isaiah 58:13).

8. _____ days ye shall gather it; (i.e. manna); but on the seventh day, which is the sabbath, in it there shall be none (Exodus 16:26).

9. And upon the first day of the week, when the _____ came together to break bread, Paul preached unto them (Acts 20:7).

10. They asked him, (i.e. Jesus) saying, Is it lawful to heal on the sabbath days? that they might _____ him (Matthew 12:10).

11. And thou shalt number seven sabbaths of _____ unto thee ... Then shalt thou cause the trumpet of the jubilee to sound. (Leviticus 25:8-9).

Honour your Parents

When a guest comes to your home, how do you treat him? Do you usher him to a comfortable chair or do you make him stand or perch on a stool? Do you listen to what he says or would you ignore him? Would you speak pleasantly to him or would you be rude? God, in his Word, the Bible, teaches us to show respect to people whether they are family, guests, schoolmates or strangers. The first people we learn to show respect to are our parents.

Children are to obey their parents in all things, for this is well pleasing to the Lord (Colossians 3:20). Children should obey their parents in the Lord, obeying only if what our parents require of us is in accordance with God's law. We should obey God rather than men (Acts 5:29). From obeying and honouring our parents we learn to pay respect to others in authority and to deal wisely with other people.

Hophni and Phinehas were wicked sons of Eli

the priest in Shiloh. They showed contempt for God's worship and lived immoral lives. When their father tried to warn them, they would not listen to him. They did not show respect to their father. This led to disaster for them and for the nation of Israel. Today we still see many people ignoring and disobeying their parents. This leads to the breakdown of the family and trouble for our nation too.

Joseph is a good example for us in showing respect for his father. He showed concern for him and lovingly provided for his needs when he settled in the land of Goshen.

Timothy listened carefully to his mother and grandmother as they taught him the Scriptures and this led him to salvation through Jesus Christ. He became a great blessing to Paul whom he helped on his journeys and to the many people to whom he preached the gospel.

But the Lord Jesus Christ is our best example. He honoured his parents perfectly. As he grew up in Nazareth he was subject to his mother and father (Luke 2:51). Even as he died on the cross, he showed concern for his mother, ensuring that his friend and disciple John looked after her in his own home (John 19:26-27). We learn from Jesus too that the honour we give to our parents is a reflection of the honour we ought to give to our heavenly Father. He is worthy of all honour and glory for ever.

Bible Verses

Honour thy father and thy mother: that thy days may be long upon the land which the LORD thy God giveth thee.
Exodus 20:12

Children, obey your parents in the Lord: for this is right.
Ephesians 6:1

My son, hear the instruction of thy father, and forsake not the law of thy mother.
Proverbs 1:8

...and his (Jesus') mother said unto him, Son, why hast thou thus dealt with us? behold, thy father and I have sought thee sorrowing.

And he said unto them, How is it that ye sought me? wist ye not that I must be about my Father's business? And they understood not the saying which he spake unto them. And he went down with them, and came to Nazareth, and was subject unto them: but his mother kept all these sayings in her heart.
And Jesus increased in wisdom and stature, and in favour with God and man.

Luke 2:48-52

Bible Search 6

Find the missing words. The initials of the correct answers will spell out a word from the story.

1. A foolish son is the _____ of his father (Proverbs 19:13).

2. A wise son maketh a glad father: but a foolish son is the _____ of his mother (Proverbs 10:1).

3. Now unto the King eternal, immortal, _____, the only wise God, be honour and glory for ever and ever. Amen. (1 Timothy 1:17).

4. Honour thy father and thy mother: that thy days may be _____ upon the land which the LORD thy God giveth thee (Exodus 20:12).

5. Render therefore to all their _____: tribute to whom tribute is due; custom to whom custom; fear to whom fear; honour to whom honour (Romans 13:7).

6. Children, obey your parents in the Lord: for this is _____ (Ephesians 6:1).

7. Ye shall fear _____ man his mother, and his father, and keep my sabbaths: I am the LORD your God (Leviticus 19:3).

8. And, ye fathers, provoke not your children to wrath: but bring them up in the _____ and admonition of the Lord (Ephesians 6:4).

Respect for Life

If you ever watch a news bulletin on television or open a newspaper, you will most likely find a story about someone being killed violently. Many horrific crimes happen in our country every day and when someone is killed we are appalled and horrified. Life is precious. God is the giver of life and no one has the right to take away life carelessly. We have been made in the image of God, and so human life is sacred.

The murderer is guilty of breaking one of God's commandments – 'You shall not kill'. But the commandment goes much further than forbidding the act of murder. The Lord Jesus in the Sermon on the Mount gave it a deeper meaning. All sins that lead to murder and are the causes of murder are also forbidden. Anger and hatred are against this law of God.

The first family was affected by the evil of murder. Adam and Eve had two sons, Cain and Abel. Abel was a shepherd and Cain cultivated the land. One day they both brought offerings to God. Cain brought some produce from the land. Abel brought one of his best animals. God was pleased with Abel's offering, but Cain's offering was not what God required. Cain was angry with God and with his brother. When the brothers were out in the field, Cain killed his brother Abel. God knew what Cain had done and he punished him by driving him out of the land. The sin of hatred led to the sin of murder.

King Saul, the first king of Israel was jealous of David who had been anointed and chosen by God to be king. Saul tried to kill David, but David escaped with the help of his dear friend Jonathan. David roamed as a fugitive in the mountains and wilderness. God kept him safe. One day, Saul came to the entrance of a cave where David was hiding. Saul settled down to sleep. David could easily have killed Saul, but he refused to do so. He secretly cut off a corner of Saul's robe. When Saul left the cave, David called after him, 'My Lord the King!' David bowed to the ground and said, 'Don't listen when people say that David wants to harm you. I could have killed you today but I spared your life.' On this occasion David obeyed the command, 'You shall not kill.'

The Bible makes it clear to us too that there are occasions when taking someone's life is not against the sixth commandment. The death penalty was laid down in the law as the just punishment for certain offences. Defending oneself and one's country in time of war is also a just reason for taking life.

God also made an exception for the person who killed someone accidentally. Six cities of refuge were set up as a place of refuge, so that revenge would not be taken on the person who killed by accident. These cities point us to the safety we find in the Lord Jesus.

Bible Verse

Thou shalt not kill.
Exodus 20:13

The murderer rising with the light killeth the poor and needy, and in the night is as a thief.
Job 24:14

For out of the heart proceed evil thoughts, murders, adulteries, fornications, thefts, false witness, blasphemies:
Matthew 15:19

Whosoever hateth his brother is a murderer: and ye know that no murderer hath eternal life abiding in him.
1 John 3:15

Bible Search 7

The initial letters of missing words from these verses.
will spell out an important word.

1. That as sin hath reigned unto death, even so
    might grace reign through _____
    unto eternal life by Jesus Christ our Lord
    (Romans 5:21).

2. And I give unto them _____ life; and they
    shall never perish (John 10:28).

3. Wherefore hast thou _____ the commandment
    of the Lord, to do evil in his sight? Thou hast killed
    Uriah the Hittite with the sword (2 Samuel 12:9).

4. He that saith he is in the light, and hateth his brother,
    is in darkness _____ until now (1 John 2:9).

5. And the Lord set a _____ upon Cain, lest any
    finding him should kill him (Genesis 4:15).

6. For, behold, the Lord cometh out of his place to
    _____ the inhabitants of the earth for
    their iniquity (Isaiah 26:21).

50

7. And Saul, yet breathing out _____ and slaughter against the disciples of the Lord, went unto the high priest (Acts 9:1).

8. Whoso sheddeth man's blood, by man shall his blood be shed: for in the _____ of God made he man (Genesis 9:6).

9. For whosoever shall keep the whole law, and yet _____ in one point, he is guilty of all (James 2:10).

10. And the LORD God formed man of the dust of the ground, and breathed into his _____ the breath of life; and man became a living soul (Genesis 2:7).

A Special Promise

Have you ever been to a wedding? It is a very happy time to see the beautiful bride and the handsome groom. Everyone gets dressed in their best and enjoys a lovely meal, celebrating with family and friends. The most important part of the wedding day is the promise the bride and groom make to each other before God and the witnesses looking on. They promise to be faithful to one another for as long as they both live.

Marriage was founded by God in the Garden of Eden when he created Eve as a wife for Adam. Adam needed support and help which he got from Eve. The family unit is a blessing from God for both adults and children.

The sin of adultery is against God and his law. When someone puts a third person in the special relationship only meant for the marriage partner, they are wronging not only the marriage partner, but God too. The commandment forbids not only actual adultery, but also impure thoughts and words.

King David fell into the sin of adultery. He stayed at home instead of going to battle with his soldiers. As he looked out from his palace roof he noticed a beautiful woman having a bath. David decided that he wanted that woman even after he found out that she was Bathsheba, the wife of Uriah, one of his soldiers. He brought her to his palace that evening. Sometime later, Bathsheba sent word to David that she was expecting a baby. In a panic David tried to cover up his sin. When Uriah refused to leave his men at the battlefield and come home, David arranged for him to be placed in the forefront of the fighting, where he was bound to get killed. Bathsheba was then free to marry David. God was displeased with David's sin – adultery leading to deceit and murder.

Nathan the prophet confronted David with his sin and this led to his repentance and forgiveness. At this time David wrote Psalm 51, confessing his sin and seeking God's cleansing and forgiveness.

When Joseph was a slave in Egypt, working in Potiphar's house, Potiphar's wife tried to entice Joseph into the sin of adultery. Joseph was given the grace to refuse. 'How could I do such a wicked thing and sin against God?' he said. Day after day Joseph refused her advances, until he had to flee from the house right away from her. She told wicked lies about Joseph which resulted in him going to prison.

But God was with Joseph and showed him mercy and gave him a favoured position in the prison.

In Paul's letter to Timothy, he advises him to flee youthful lusts and instead to follow righteousness, faith, charity, peace from a pure heart. That is good advice for us too. God's commandment extends to our heart, mind and imagination as well as our actions.

The sanctity of marriage is emphasised when Paul speaks about the relationship between the Lord Jesus Christ and his church. The husband is the head of the wife, just as Christ is the head of the church. Husbands are told to love their wives just as Christ loved the church.

We should pray that the Lord will keep us close to himself and pure in thought, word and deed.

Bible Verses

Thou shalt not commit adultery.
Exodus 20:14

Wives, submit yourselves unto your own husbands, as unto the Lord. For the husband is the head of the wife, even as Christ is the head of the church: and he is the saviour of the body. Therefore as the church is subject unto Christ, so let the wives be to their own husbands in every thing. Husbands, love your wives, even as Christ also loved the church, and gave himself for it; That he might sanctify and cleanse it with the washing of water by the word, That he might present it to himself a glorious church, not having spot,

or wrinkle, or any such thing; but that it should be holy and without blemish. So ought men to love their wives as their own bodies. He that loveth his wife loveth himself. For no man ever yet hated his own flesh; but nourisheth and cherisheth it, even as the Lord the church:
Ephesians 5:22-29

Bible Search 8

Find the missing word. The initial letters of the correct answers will spell out a word from the story.

1. Have _____ upon me, O God, according to thy lovingkindness (Psalm 51:1).

2. What therefore God hath joined together, let not man put _____ (Matthew 19:6).

3. As the bridegroom rejoiceth over the bride, so shall thy God _____ over thee (Isaiah 62:5).

4. Let us be glad and rejoice, and give honour to him: for the marriage of the Lamb is come, and his wife hath made herself _____ (Revelation 19:7).

5. _____ not my heart to any evil thing, to practise wicked works with men that work iniquity (Psalm 141:4).

6. But I say unto you, That whosoever looketh on a woman to lust after her hath committed _____ with her already in his heart (Matthew 5:28).

7. Husbands, love your wives, even as Christ also loved the church, and _____ himself for it (Ephesians 5:25).

8. Stand fast therefore in the liberty wherewith Christ hath made us free, and be not _____ again with the yoke of bondage (Galatians 5:1).

Respect for Property

If you found a purse with money in it lying on the road, what would you do? If you knocked over a box of buttons on your mother's table and a £1 coin rolled out, what would you do?

God wants us to be honest and true in our dealings with others. If we cheat or steal, no one may ever find out, but God always knows. One of his commands says, 'You shall not steal.'

God gave Joshua and the people of Israel an amazing victory over the city of Jericho. The people were told that all the silver and gold and valuable things in Jericho belonged to the Lord. One man, Achan, stole some silver and gold and clothes for himself. He hid them in the ground under his tent.

Nobody saw it, but God had seen what he had done. God can see everything we do too. Nothing is hidden from him.

Achan's stealing brought a lot of trouble to Israel. The next city Joshua was to conquer was Ai. The Israelites thought that would be quite easy, but they got a terrible shock. The men of Ai won the battle and chased them away. Joshua was very upset about this defeat and asked God why it had happened. God told him that someone in the camp had sinned by stealing some of the precious things that belonged to the Lord.

Early next morning Joshua, with God's guidance, found out which tribe was guilty, then which clan, then which family. Finally Achan was singled out to be the guilty one. He was severely punished for this sin. The people threw stones at him until he died. The next attempt to take the city of Ai was successful.

Zacchaeus was a thief too. His job was collecting tax money for the government, but he overcharged the people and kept the extra for himself. Nobody liked him.

One day Jesus came to his town, Jericho. Zacchaeus wanted to see Jesus, but the crowds were so large and Zacchaeus was too short to see over their heads. Instead he climbed up a sycamore tree to get a good view. Jesus spotted him. 'Come down, Zacchaeus,' he said. 'I want to visit your house today.'

Zacchaeus welcomed Jesus to his house and this visit changed Zacchaeus' life. 'I will give half my possessions to the poor,' he said. 'If I have cheated anyone, I will pay back four times as much.'

'Today salvation has come to this house,' said Jesus. Zacchaeus' sin was forgiven and his life was turned around. He was now obeying the command 'You shall not steal,' instead of disobeying it.

The reason for the big difference was the Lord Jesus Christ, who kept all the law of God perfectly. We cannot keep God's law perfectly, but if we repent of our sin and trust in Jesus Christ who died on the cross in our place, then God accepts us as righteous in his sight.

Bible Verses

Thou shalt not steal.
Exodus 20:15

Ye shall not steal, neither deal
falsely, neither lie one to another.
Leviticus 19:11

Lay not up for yourselves treasures
upon earth, where moth and rust
doth corrupt, and where thieves
break through and steal. But lay up
for yourselves treasures in heaven,
where neither moth nor rust doth
corrupt, and where thieves do not
break through nor steal.
Matthew 6:19-20

Bible Search 9

Find the missing words from the texts. The initial letters of your answers will spell out the subject of the story.

1. Recompense to no man evil for evil. _____ things honest in the sight of all men (Romans 12:17).

2. The wicked borroweth, and payeth not again: but the _____ sheweth mercy, and giveth (Psalm 37:21).

3. If thou sell ought unto thy neighbour, or buyest ought of thy neighbour's hand, ye shall not _____ one another (Leviticus 25:14).

4. Whoso is _____ with a thief hateth his own soul (Proverbs 29:24).

5. Let no man seek his own, but _____ man another's wealth (1 Corinthians 10:24).

6. Let him that stole steal no more: but _____ let him labour, working with his hands the thing

which is good, that he may have to give to him that needeth (Ephesians 4:28).

7. For out of the heart proceed evil thoughts, murders, adulteries, fornications, _____, false witness, blasphemies (Matthew 15:19).

8. Stand fast therefore in the liberty wherewith Christ hath made us free, and be not entangled again with the _____ of bondage (Galatians 5:1).

Tell the Truth

Have you ever told a lie to get out of trouble? 'No, I didn't touch that,' when you did. Or, 'But I have done my homework,' when you haven't. God hates lying and warns us against it in his Word.

The Bible tells us in the book of James that the tongue is a very small part of our body, but can do a great deal of harm. The words that we say can cause pain and trouble to ourselves and others. We all make mistakes and often say things that are wrong. Deliberate lying and deceit is against God's holy law.

If someone is called to be a witness in court, he must promise to tell the truth, the whole truth and nothing but the truth – not hiding any of the facts or adding in things that did not happen. It is a crime to be a false witness in court.

God has commanded us to tell the truth at all times, even if it makes us unpopular. Micaiah was a prophet of the Lord, a man who spoke God's message. King Ahab wanted advice about going to war against Syria, but he only listened to those who said he would win. Micaiah was sent for by the king. Someone told him, 'All the others have prophesied success for the king; you should do the same.' Micaiah answered, 'I will say what the Lord tells me.' Micaiah told the truth. He foretold disaster. Ahab did not like the truth and

ordered Micaiah to be thrown in prison on a diet of bread and water. All Micaiah had done was speak the truth, even when it was difficult. Micaiah wanted to obey God's commandment about telling the truth.

Gehazi was the servant of Elisha the man of God. Elisha was used by God to heal the leprosy of Naaman the Syrian army captain. Naaman wanted to give a token of thanks to Elisha, but he refused. Later, Gehazi decided to chase after Naaman. He made up a story about visitors coming to Elisha's house and he would now accept some silver and clothes for them. Naaman gave him even more than he asked. Gehazi came back home and hid the money.

When Elisha challenged him he said, 'I haven't been anywhere.' But God had revealed to Elisha what Gehazi had done. Because of his lying and deceit, Gehazi was punished with leprosy, the same disease as Naaman.

Lying is a serious sin which God hates. It deserves God's wrath and curse. But the glory of the gospel is the Jesus Christ came to this world to bear our sin in his own body on the cross.

God is the God of truth. Jesus described him as the only true God. He does not lie.

One of the names of Jesus is 'the truth'. 'I am the way, the truth and the life,' he said (John 14:6). All that Jesus said was true. 'He did no sin, neither was guile found in his mouth' (1 Peter 2:22).

The Bible is true. Every word is from God and can be trusted completely. God wants us to believe it and obey it.

Bible Verses

Thou shalt not bear false witness
against thy neighbour.
Exodus 20:16

He that speaketh truth sheweth forth
righteousness:
but a false witness deceit.
Proverbs 12:17

The lip of truth shall be established
for ever: but a lying tongue is but for
a moment.
Proverbs 12:19

These are the things that ye shall do; Speak ye every man the truth to his neighbour; execute the judgment of truth and peace in your gates: And let none of you imagine evil in your hearts against his neighbour; and love no false oath: for all these are things that I hate, saith the Lord.
Zechariah 8:16-17

Bible Search 10

Find the missing words from the text. The initial letters of the correct answers will spell out the topic of the story.

1. Jesus saith unto him, I am the way, the _____ and the life: no man cometh unto the Father, but by me (John 14:6).

2. Be not _____ with thy mouth and let not thine heart be hasty to utter any thing before God ... (Ecclesiastes 5:2).

3. He that walketh _____ and, worketh righteousness, and speaketh the truth in his heart (Psalm 15:2).

4. Let not mercy and truth forsake thee: bind them about thy neck; write them upon the _____ of thine heart (Proverbs 3:3).

5. Every one that is of the truth _____ my voice (John 18:37).

6. They speak vanity every one with his neighbour: with _____ lips and with a double heart do they speak (Psalm 12:2).

7. Then said I, Woe is me! For I am _____; because I am a man of unclean lips, and I dwell in the midst of a people of unclean lips (Isaiah 6:5).

8. Wherefore putting away _____, speak every man truth with his neighbour: for we are members one of another (Ephesians 4:25).

9. Speak ye every man the truth to his _____ (Zechariah 8:16).

10. _____ the judgement of truth and peace in your gates (Zechariah 8:16).

11. Deliver my _____, O LORD, from lying lips, and from a deceitful tongue (Psalm 120:2).

12. Keep thy tongue from evil, and thy lips from _____ guile (Psalm 34:13).

Learn to be Content

Sometimes we can feel unhappy because we would like to be better looking or more clever. Do you ever wish that you had the same bike or game as your friend? God tells us that wanting what others have and not being content with how God has made us, is the sin of covetousness. God has commanded us not to covet anything that is our neighbour's. How often we forget that. We envy others and are not content with what we have.

The children of Israel were wonderfully provided for by God. They were miraculously delivered from slavery in Egypt. But soon they began to murmur and complain. They complained to Moses at Marah because the water was not sweet and God graciously heard Moses' prayer and the Lord showed Moses a tree to throw into the water which was then drinkable.

Then they complained of hunger. 'We were better off in Egypt. We had plenty of food there.' They forgot the slavery and misery that God had saved them from. God graciously provided bread from heaven for them – the manna which appeared on the ground six days a week with a double portion on the sixth day which gave sufficient for the sabbath too. Soon they grew tired of this marvellous provision and longed for the fish and melons, cucumbers and vegetables they had in Egypt.

Do we complain about our God-given situation like the Israelites? Do we forget the deliverance from slavery to sin that the Lord Jesus Christ procured for us on the cross? Are we too absorbed by worldly possessions and comforts? The Lord has promised never to leave or forsake his people. That should make us very content. Even when things are difficult, the Lord wants us to trust him and look to him for help.

The apostle Paul had a very arduous and difficult life, enduring hardships and persecution. He could say that he had learned to be content whatever his circumstances. The Lord Jesus Christ was the strength of his life, who helped him to have a right perspective on his situation. 'I can do all things through Christ who strengthens me,' he said. Contentment was something Paul had to learn. It did not come naturally.

Our heavenly Father knows what we need. Our duty is to seek first the kingdom of God and his righteousness and to trust God to provide what he knows is best for us. We know that all things work together for good to them that love God, to them who are the called according to his purpose (Romans 8:28).

Bible Verses

Thou shalt not covet thy neighbour's house, thou shalt not covet thy neighbour's wife, nor his manservant, nor his maidservant, nor his ox, nor his ass, nor any thing that is thy neighbour's.
Exodus 20:17

Incline my heart unto thy testimonies, and not to covetousness.
Psalm 119:36

The prince that wanteth understanding is also a great oppressor: but he that hateth covetousness shall prolong his days.
Proverbs 28:16

And he said unto them, Take heed, and beware of covetousness: for a man's life consisteth not in the abundance of the things which he possesseth.
Luke 12:15

Let your conversation be without covetousness; and be content with such things as ye have: for he hath said, I will never leave thee, nor forsake thee.
Hebrews 13:5

Bible Search 11

Look up the verse and find the missing word. The initial letters of your answers will spell out a word which should describe us if we are trusting in God.

1. I can do all things through _____ which strengtheneth me (Philippians 4:13).

2. The prince that wanteth understanding is also a great _____: but he that hateth covetousness shall prolong his days (Proverbs 28:16).

3. Yea, ye yourselves know, that these hands have ministered unto my _____ , and to them that were with me (Acts 20:34).

4. Let your conversation be without covetousness; and be content with such _____ as ye have: for he hath said, I will never leave thee nor forsake thee (Hebrews 13:5).

5. Take therefore no thought for the morrow: for the morrow shall take thought for the things of itself.

Sufficient unto the day is the _____ thereof (Matthew 6:34).

6. I know both how to be abased, and I know how to abound: every where and in all things I am instructed both to be full and to be hungry, both to abound and to suffer _____ (Philippians 4:12).

7. And having food and raiment let us be _____ content (1 Timothy 6:8).

8. For where _____ and strife is, there is confusion and every evil work (James 3:16).

9. Delight thyself also in the Lord; and he shall give thee the _____ of thine heart (Psalm 37:4).

Jesus and the Ten Commandments

The Ten Commandments are God's guidelines for daily living. God gave them to Moses on Mount Sinai thousands of years ago, but they apply to us today.

One day a Pharisee, who was a lawyer, tried to catch Jesus out. He asked, 'Which is the great commandment in the law?'

'Thou shalt love the Lord thy God with all thy heart, and with all thy soul and with all thy mind,' Jesus replied. 'And the second is, Thou shalt love thy neighbour as thyself.'

These two statements sum up the whole law. Love for God will lead to worshipping him only, in the way that he has set down in his Word. Loving God will mean that we use his name reverently and keep his day holy.

Loving others as ourselves will cause us to honour our parents, to be careful about others' life, purity and property. The whole of God's commandments is summed up by the word – love.

Jesus is the only person who ever kept the law perfectly. Jesus loved God his Father and obeyed him perfectly even although that meant death on a cross. He loved his people too. He loved them so much that he laid down his life for them, bearing their sin. The Bible says that there is no greater love shown than when someone gives their life for a friend. Jesus showed the greatest love by dying for sinners.

Jesus kept the law perfectly. He always did what pleased God his Father. He worshipped God in the right way – going regularly to the synagogue and praying often in private. He kept the sabbath day holy – using it for worshipping God and helping the needy. He honoured his parents. Even when dying on the cross he made sure that his mother would be looked after by his friend, John. He was kind and loving. His thoughts, words and actions were pure and good.

We cannot keep the law as Jesus did, but because he took our place and punishment on the cross, God accepts us as righteous in his sight. Those who live and trust Jesus do not keep the commandments to earn a place in heaven. Their place in heaven is secure because of what Jesus did when he died on the cross in their place. He rose again to show his power over death.

Christians want to show their love for Christ. 'If you love me, keep my commandments,' Jesus said. Pray that the Lord will keep you from falling and will present you faultless before the presence of his glory with exceeding joy (Jude 24), not because of your goodness, but because of the finished work of the Lord Jesus for his people.

Bible Verses

Now unto him that is able to keep
you from falling, and to present you
faultless before the presence of his
glory with exceeding joy,
to the only wise God our Saviour,
be glory and majesty, dominion and
power, both now and ever. Amen.
Jude 24-25

For we have not an high priest which
cannot be touched with the feeling of
our infirmities; but was in all points
tempted like as we are,
yet without sin.
Hebrews 4:15

So Christ was once offered to bear
the sins of many; and unto them
that look for him shall he appear the
second time without sin
unto salvation.
Hebrews 9:28

For he hath made him to be sin for
us, who knew no sin; that we might be
made the righteousness
of God in him.
2 Corinthians 5:21

Bible Search 12

Find the missing words. The initials of your answers will spell out the subject of the story.

1. These are the words which I spake unto you, while I was yet with you, that all things must be fulfilled, which were written in the law of Moses, and in the prophets and in the psalms, _____ me (Luke 24:44).

2. Only be thou strong and very courageous, that thou mayest _____ to do according to all the law, which Moses my servant commanded thee (Joshua 1:7).

3. Let us hear the conclusion of the whole _____: Fear God, and keep his commandments: for this is the whole duty of man (Ecclesiastes 12:13).

4. Now we know that what things soever the law saith, it saith to them who are under the law: that

every _____ may be stopped, and all the world may become guilty before God (Romans 3:19).

5. He ... and _____ a law in Israel, which he commanded our fathers, that they should make them known to their children (Psalm 78:5).

6. But the word is very _____ unto thee, in thy mouth, and in thy heart, that thou mayest do it (Deuteronomy 30:14).

7. O that my ways were _____ to keep thy statutes! (Psalm 119:5)

8. To the Lord our God belong _____ and forgivenesses, though we have rebelled against him (Daniel 9:9).

9. Because the carnal mind is _____ against God: for it is not subject to the law of God, neither indeed can be (Romans 8:7).

10. If ye fulfil the royal law according to the scripture, Thou shalt love thy _____ as thyself, ye do well (James 2:8).

11. _____ not that I am come to destroy the law, or the prophets: I am not come to destroy, but to fulfil (Matthew 5:17).

12. For we know that the law is _____: but I am carnal, sold under sin (Romans 7:14).

The Author

Carine Mackenzie has written over one hundred and fifty books for children. She has a talent for retelling Bible stories that has meant that children from all over the world have been given the opportunity to discover Jesus Christ for themselves.

Carine's writing started when she and her husband saw a need for children's books that retold Bible stories accurately. They had three young daughters who loved stories. Carine and her husband longed for them to come to know the Saviour who died for them on the cross. They also wanted their children to apply the truth of the Bible to their own lives.

So one day, in the kitchen of her house in Inverness, Carine sat down to write her first two books – *Gideon: the Soldier of God* and *Mary: the Mother of Jesus*.

Her 150th book was published in 2011 – *365 Great Bible Stories: The Good News of Jesus Christ from Genesis to Revelation*.

With sales of over three million books worldwide, Carine continues to write books for children. It's not just her children who inspire her now to write books, but her young grandchildren who love stories just as much as the previous generation.

Answers

Bible Search 1
seek, first, the kingdom, of God, and his, righteousness.

Bible Search 2
whole, only, rejoice, sinned, humbly, into, presence, golden, obey, direct. **Worship God.**

Bible Search 3
images, dearly, obey, lips, add, turned, rebellion, yield. **Idolatry.**

Bible Search 4
salvation, terrible, rejoice, offering, needy, generations, truth, other, wait, exalted, righteousness. **Strong tower.**

Bible Search 5
throughout, hand, evil, labour, omega, rested, delight, six, disciples, accuse, years. **The Lord's Day.**

Bible Search 6
calamity, heaviness, invisible, long, dues, right, every, nurture. **Children.**

Bible Search 7
righteousness, eternal, despised, even, mark, punish, threatenings, image, offend, nostrils. **Redemption.**

Bible Search 8
mercy, asunder, rejoice, ready, incline, adultery, gave, entangled. **Marriage.**

Bible Search 9
provide, righteous, oppress, partner, every, rather, thefts, yoke. **Property.**

Bible Search 10
truth, rash, uprightly, table, heareth, flattering, undone, lying, neighbour, execute, soul, speaking. **Truthfulness.**

Bible Search 11
Christ, oppressor, necessities, things, evil, need, therewith, envying, desires. **Contented.**

Bible Search 12
concerning, observe, matter, mouth, appointed, nigh, directed, mercies, enmity, neighbour, think, spiritual. **Commandments.**

Following God
by Carine Mackenzie

If you were standing underneath a plum tree you wouldn't expect to see bananas hanging there. If you reached up into the leaves of an apple tree you wouldn't pull down a coconut on top of your head. That just wouldn't happen. You know what sort of tree it is by its fruit and the Bible says that you know if someone is a Christian or not by the fruit of their lives. What sort of fruit is that?... well there is one fruit that is produced in a Christian and that is the Fruit of the Spirit. Find out about the different parts of this fruit by reading this book... and by reading Galatians Chapter 5 from the Bible.

ISBN: 978-1-84550-750-3

Carine MacKenzie

Trusting God
by Carine Mackenzie

Do you know what your name means? Each year a list is compiled of the popular names given to babies born in that year. The list changes slightly year on year. God has many names that are truly unique. Carine has taken seven of God's names to explain them for children aged 7-11 years. Using a Bible story, she shows them how these names of God are still relevant to us today. Your children will be fascinated by these new words.

ISBN: 978-1-84550-271-3